SPORTS QUESTION AND ANSWER BOOK

SPORTS QUESTION AND ANSWER BOOK

By Bill Adler

Illustrations by ED MALSBERG

Publishers · GROSSET & DUNLAP · New York
A FILMWAYS COMPANY

Copyright © 1978 by Bill Adler
All Rights Reserved
Library of Congress Catalog Card Number: 77-85636
ISBN: 0-448-14295-3 (Paperback Edition)
ISBN: 0-448-13064-5 (Library Edition)
Published Simultaneously in Canada
Printed in the United States of America

When did the Davis Cup tennis matches start? Was it 1906, 1908, or 1900?

The Davis Cup matches began in 1900, with the American tennis team easily beating the team from Great Britain.

True or false? Baseball player Jackie Robinson was once voted Rookie of the Year.

True. Jackie Robinson, playing for the Brooklyn Dodgers, was voted Rookie of the Year in 1947.

Jackie Robinson

Which relief pitcher holds the record for pitching the most innings in one season?

Mike Marshall, playing for the Los Angeles Dodgers in 1974, pitched a record-breaking 208 innings.

When did Chris Evert win her first singles championship at Forest Hills?

The year was 1975.

Chris Evert

Vince Lombardi was the great coach of the Green Bay Packers. True or false?

True.

Vince Lombardi

Bjorn Borg

True or false? Bjorn Borg won the men's singles at Wimbledon in 1976.

True. Sweden's Bjorn Borg beat Ilie Nastase, of Romania, 6–4, 6–2, 9–7.

Name the team that won the Women's Professional Softball Association World Series in 1976.

Connecticut beat San José.

In 1970, 1972, and 1974 the same baseball player for the Cincinnati Reds led the National League in runs batted in. Who was he?

Johnny Bench batted in 148 runs in 1970, 125 in 1972, and 129 in 1974.

Which professional softball player is considered the greatest woman softball pitcher?

Joan Joyce, of the Connecticut Falcons. In the 1976 season she won thirty-nine games and lost only two.

Which baseball league has a "designated hitter"?

The American League.

Stan Musial

What was the first year that Stan Musial won the National League batting championship? Was it 1941, 1942, or 1943?

The right answer is 1943. In that year Stan Musial, playing for the St. Louis Cardinals, led the National League in batting with an average of .357. Musial also led the National League in batting in 1946, 1948, 1950, 1951, and 1952.

Don Drysdale was a great pitcher for the Los Angeles Dodgers. What record does he hold?

Don Drysdale pitched the most consecutive shutouts while pitching for Los Angeles between May 14 and June 4, 1968. Drysdale also holds the record for the most consecutive scoreless innings in one season. He had 58 between May 14 and June 8, 1968.

Can you name the professional baseball player who had the most hits in one season? Was it Joe DiMaggio, Ty Cobb, Babe Ruth, or George Sisler?

In 1920, while playing for St. Louis in the American League, George Sisler had 257 hits.

Who was the last American man to become the world champion figure skater

In 1970, Tim Wood was the world champion figure skater in the men's division. Wood also won in 1969.

True or false? The men's American swimming team won twelve out of a possible thirteen gold medals in the 1976 Olympics.

True.

Who was the professional quarterback who completed the most passes in a single game?

George Blanda, in a game between Houston and Buffalo on November 1, 1964, completed 37 passes.

Who was the first major-league baseball umpire to wear glasses?

Ed Rommel, in 1956.

The man who calls the balls and strikes behind the plate in a baseball game is called: (1) referee; (2) umpire; (3) coach.

The right answer is (2) umpire.

Babe Ruth was the most famous New York Yankee of all time. Which team did he play for before he became a Yankee?

The great Babe Ruth was a pitcher and outfielder for the Boston Red Sox from 1914 to 1919.

Which baseball manager holds the record for the most consecutive league championships?

Casey Stengel, who led the New York Yankees to five American League pennants, in 1949, 1950, 1951, 1952, and 1953.

Which was the first city in Canada to have a major-league baseball team? Montreal or Toronto?

Montreal.

What do these professional football players have in common? Y.A. Tittle, Joe Kapp, Adrian Burk, Sid Luckman, and George Blanda.

Each has thrown 7 touchdown passes in a single game.

Kareem Abdul-Jabbar

In the 1976–1977 NBL basketball season, the Most Valuable Player Award went to Kareem Abdul-Jabbar of the Los Angeles Lakers. Who won that award in the 1975–1976 season?

Kareem Abdul-Jabbar.

Put on your thinking cap. Can you name the pitcher who pitched two no-hitters in a row?

Johnny Vander Meer pitched no-hitters for Cincinnati on June 11 and June 15, 1938.

Which professional football team was known as the "Fearsome Foursome"?

The Los Angeles Rams' defensive line of the early 1960's. The line consisted of tackles Merlin Olsen and Roosevelt Grier and ends Lamar Lundy and Deacon Jones.

Name the swimmer who holds the world record for the 100-meter butterfly stroke.

Mark Spitz. His time for the 100-meter butterfly at the Summer Olympics in Munich was 54.27 on August 31, 1972.

Helen Wills Moody

True or false? Helen Wills Moody was the only woman to win the Wimbledon tennis singles title eight times.

True. Ms. Moody won the Wimbledon in 1927, 1928, 1929, 1930, 1932, 1933, 1935, and 1938.

Who was the first baseball player to receive $100,000 a year?

In 1949 New York Yankee Joe DiMaggio was paid $100,000. The first football player to earn $100,000 was Johnny Unitas.

Which professional hockey team won the Stanley Cup for the most consecutive years?

The Montreal Canadiens won the Stanley Cup every year from 1955-1956 through 1959-1960.

Was it Tom Seaver or Nolan Ryan who had the most consecutive strikeouts in one game?

If you said Tom Seaver, you were right. Tom "Terrific," who now pitches for the Cincinnati Reds, had ten strikeouts in a row while pitching for the New York Mets against San Diego on April 22, 1970.

Name the professional football player who scored the most points in a single season. Was it Johnny Unitas, Paul Hornung, Joe Namath, or George Blanda?

Paul Hornung scored 176 points, playing for Green Bay in 1960.

Which professional football team has won the most league championships?

The Green Bay Packers. The Packers won their league championship eleven times—from 1929 to 1931, 1936, 1939, 1944, 1961, 1962, and 1965 to 1967.

Which was the first American hockey team to compete in the National Hockey League?

The Boston Bruins, when they joined the NHL in 1924.

True or false? The basketball player with the most rebounds in one season was Spencer Haywood.

False. Wilt Chamberlain had the most rebounds in one season—2,149 rebounds for Philadelphia during the 1960–1961 season.

True or false? Table tennis, also known as Ping Pong, is a national sport in China.

True.

Which baseball player holds the record for the most stolen bases? Is it Ty Cobb?

The great Ty Cobb stole 892 bases during his career, but that wasn't the record. The record is held by Billy Hamilton, who stole 937 bases while playing for Kansas City, Philadelphia, and Boston. Billy Hamilton started his professional baseball career in 1888 and retired in 1908.

Which basketball teams played in the first basketball game ever televised?

A game between Pittsburgh and Fordham was televised from Madison Square Garden on February 28, 1940.

Billie Jean King

True or false? Billie Jean King won the championship at Wimbledon six times?

True. The great tennis star won the Wimbledon tournaments from 1966 to 1968, 1972, 1973, and 1975.

In which city will you find the Orange Bowl? Is it Miami, New Orleans, Dallas, or Memphis?

The Orange Bowl is located in Miami, Florida.

Who were the two professional baseball players who stole home 7 times in one season?

Pete Reiser for Brooklyn, in 1946, and Rod Carew for Minnesota, in 1969.

Wilt Chamberlain   Walt Frazier   Elgin Baylor   Bill Walton

Name the professional basketball player who scored the most points in one game in an NBA championship series. Was it Wilt Chamberlain, Walt Frazier, Elgin Baylor, or Bill Walton?

If you said Wilt Chamberlain, you were right. Chamberlain scored 100 points in a championship game between Philadelphia and New York on March 2, 1962.

The horse that won the Kentucky Derby in 1977 was Seattle Slew. True or false?

True.

How many events are there in a Decathlon? Are there eight, nine, ten, or twelve?

The right answer is ten.

Between 1967 and 1975 one college basketball team won the NCAA championship every year except one. Name that team.

UCLA won the NCAA championship every year from 1967 to 1975 except for 1974, when the championship went to North Carolina State.

True or false? The Summer Olympic Games have never been held in the United States.

False. The Summer Olympic Games were held in St. Louis, Missouri, in 1904 and in Los Angeles, California, in 1932.

True or false? The game of La Crosse started in Canada.

True.

At the 1976 Winter Olympics one country placed first in all the bobsledding events. Which country was it? West Germany, East Germany, or Switzerland?

East Germany.

Lou Gehrig

True or false? Lou Gehrig was a great baseball player, but he also played football for Columbia University?

True. Gehrig played fullback for Columbia in 1922.

Rick Wohlhuter

Which runner holds the record for the half mile?

Former Notre Dame track star Rick Wohlhuter ran the half mile in 1:44.1 on June 8, 1974, at the Heyward Field Restoration Track and Field Meet at Eugene, Oregon.

Which professional football player holds the record for the most passes caught?

Charlie Taylor, of the Washington Redskins, caught 635 passes.

Which stadium was known as "the house that Ruth built"?

Yankee Stadium, where Babe Ruth played during his fabulous career.

Can you name the player who led the American League in batting in 1976?

George Brett, playing for Kansas City, had a batting average of .333.

Who is the all-time money winner among professional bowlers?

Dick Weber, from St. Louis, Missouri, won $519,943 as a professional bowler.

Did a professional football team ever have a team psychiatrist?

Yes. During the 1972 and 1973 seasons Dr. Arnold Mandell, professor of psychiatry at the University of California, San Diego, was an inside observer of the San Diego Chargers.

True or false? Ted Williams, the great Boston Red Sox star, hit over .400.

True. Ted Williams hit .406 for the Boston Red Sox in 1941.

Ted Williams

Name the sites of the last three Summer Olympics.

The 1968 Summer Olympics were held in Mexico City, Mexico. The 1972 Summer Olympics were held in Munich, West Germany, and the 1976 Summer Olympics were held in Montreal, Canada.

Rick Barry is an exciting professional athlete. Is he a football player, a basketball player, or a hockey player?

Barry plays basketball for the Golden State Warriors.

Who was the great golfer who won the British Open title six times between 1896 and 1914? Was it Bobby Jones?

The correct answer is Harry Vardon. In addition to the British Open, Harry Vardon won the U.S. Open in 1900.

How fast can the puck go in a professional hockey game? Is it 30 miles an hour, 90 miles an hour, 110 miles an hour, or 185 miles an hour?

The great hockey player Bobby Hull hit a hockey puck that went 185 miles an hour.

What was the longest professional boxing match?

A middleweight fight between Andy Bowen and Jack Burke lasted 110 rounds in New Orleans in 1893. The fight lasted seven hours and nineteen minutes, and it was a draw.

Which team won the 1977 Super Bowl game?

The Oakland Raiders defeated the Minnesota Vikings, 32 to 14.

When was the last time the New York Rangers hockey team won the Stanley Cup?

The Rangers won the Stanley Cup in the 1939–1940 hockey season.

Who was the great professional football player who played twenty-five seasons?

George Blanda. Blanda started his career in 1949 with the Chicago Bears.

Which professional golfer was the PGA's leading money winner five times between 1971 and 1976? Was it Jack Nicklaus, Johnny Miller, or Arnold Palmer?

The correct answer is Jack Nicklaus. He was the leading money winner every year from 1971 to 1976 except for 1974, when Johnny Miller was the PGA leading money winner.

Jack Nicklaus   *Johnny Miller*   *Arnold Palmer*

Which professional hockey team scored the most points in one season?

In the 1975–1976 season, the Montreal Canadiens of the National Hockey League scored 127 points. They won fifty-eight games, lost eleven, and tied eleven.

In which year did the great horse Whirlaway win the Kentucky Derby? Was it in 1941 or 1943?

The answer is 1941. In 1943 Count Fleet won the Kentucky Derby.

In which year did American League player Roger Maris hit 61 home runs? Was it 1960, 1961, or 1964?

The correct answer is 1961.

Only two women have ever won the tennis grand slam. Who were they?

Margaret Smith Court, of Australia, in 1970, and Maureen Connolly, of the United States, in 1953. The grand slam consists of the singles tournaments at Forest Hills and Wimbledon, and the singles titles in Australia and France.

Which professional football player had the most field goals in one season?

Jim Turner, of the New York Jets, kicked 34 field goals during the 1968 season.

True or false? The Baseball Hall of Fame is located in Brooklyn, New York.

False. The Baseball Hall of Fame is located in Cooperstown, New York.

Bold Forbes won the Kentucky Derby in 1976. Which horse placed second?

Honest Pleasure.

Only five heavyweight prize fighters retired while they were still champions. How many can you name?

The five heavyweight prize fighters who retired while they were still champions were Jim Jeffries in 1905, Jack Johnson in 1913, Gene Tunney in 1930, Joe Louis in 1949, and Rocky Marciano in 1956. Later, though, Jeffries, Johnson, and Louis lost their bids in attempted comebacks.

Who was the last American to win the Grand Prix Formula-1 world driving championship? Was it Richard Petty, Al Unser, or Phil Hill?

Phil Hill was the Grand Prix Formula-1 winner in 1961.

Which major-league baseball manager was known as Leo "the lip"?

Leo Durocher.

Leo Durocher, "the lip"

Name the professional football player who most frequently led his league in passing.

It was the great quarterback Sammy Baugh, of the Washington Redskins. He led the league in passing six times, in 1937, 1940, 1943, 1945, 1947, and 1949.

True or false? The great horse Secretariat won the Triple Crown—the Kentucky Derby, The Preakness, and the Belmont stakes.

True. Secretariat was the 1973 Triple Crown winner.

Arthur Ashe

In the 1975 tennis championship at Wimbledon, Arthur Ashe scored an upset by defeating which great tennis player? Was it Rod Laver, Stan Smith, or Jimmy Connors?

Arthur Ashe defeated Jimmy Connors, who had won at Wimbledon the year before.

Who was the Most Valuable Player in the North American Soccer League in 1976?

Pele of the New York Cosmos.

Pele

Can you guess which major-league baseball player holds the record for playing in the most games?

That record belongs to Hank Aaron, who had played in a grand total of 3,213 games by 1975.

Who holds the major-league record for the most grand-slam home runs?

Lou Gehrig, of the New York Yankees, hit 23 grand-slam homers.

Can you name the oldest man ever to win a major-league batting title?

When Ted Williams was forty years old, in 1958, he hit .328 for Boston and won the American League batting title.

Which professional baseball pitcher holds the record for pitching the most innings in a World Series game?

Believe it or not, it was the great slugger Babe Ruth, who pitched 14 innings for the Boston Red Sox in the World Series game against Brooklyn on October 9, 1916. Ruth was the winning pitcher as Boston beat Brooklyn 2 to 1.

Which baseball team is known as "The Big Red Machine"?

The Cincinnati Reds of the National League.

Who holds the world land speed record for jet-propelled automobiles?

Gary Gabelich, driving his *Blue Flame* automobile on October 23, 1970, reached an average speed of 622.07 miles per hour.

Who was Rookie of the Year in the National Basketball Association for the 1975–1976 season?

Alvan Adams, of Phoenix, was the NBA choice.

When was the first Rugby game played? Was it 1823, 1826, or 1830?

Rugby was originated in 1823 at the Rugby School in England by a student named William Ellis.

In baseball, it's the World Series. In football it's the Super Bowl. True or false?

True.

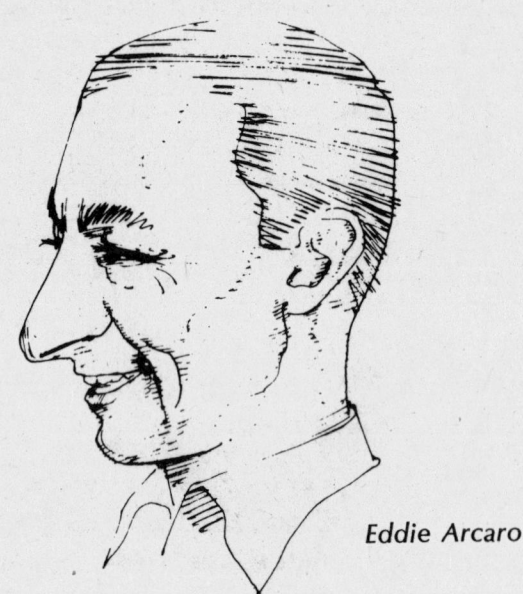
Eddie Arcaro

Eddie Arcaro was a great football player. True or false?

False. Eddie Arcaro was one of the greatest jockeys of all time.

Which major-league outfielder had the highest career fielding average?

Jimmy Piersall. His average was .990 between 1950 and 1967, when he played for six teams.

True or false? In the 1976 Olympic Games at Montreal, Canada, the United States won more gold medals than the Soviet Union.

False. The Soviet Union won forty-seven gold medals in the 1976 Olympics, and the United States won thirty-four.

Garry Unger, of St. Louis, played in more consecutive games than any professional hockey player. Did he play in 643 consecutive games, 743, or 843?

If you guessed 643, you were right.

Garry Unger

Which professional basketball player scored the most points in a single game in his rookie season?

Wilt Chamberlain scored 58 points during one game in the 1959–1960 season, when he was a rookie with the Philadelphia Warriors.

Between 1959 and 1966 one NBL basketball player was the leading scorer for each year. Who was it?

Wilt Chamberlain, playing for Philadelphia.

In which professional basketball game were the most points scored?

In an ABA game between the San Diego Conquistadors and the New York Nets on February 14, 1975, 342 points were scored. San Diego won the game, 176 to 166, with Julius Erving scoring 63 points.

Who were the last baseball players to become the unanimous choices of the Baseball Writers' Association of America as the Most Valuable Players in the National and American Leagues?

Orlando Cepeda, first baseman for St. Louis in the National League, in 1961, and Dennis McLain, a pitcher for Detroit in the American League, in 1968.

Can you name the Coach of the Year for the 1975–1976 professional basketball season?

It was Bill Fitch, who coached Cleveland.

Name the National League pitcher who completed the most games in 1976.

Randy Jones, pitching for San Diego, completed twenty-five games. In the American League, Mark Fidrych completed the most games, twenty-four, for Detroit.

Which baseball player holds the record for batting safely in the most consecutive games?

Joe DiMaggio. The New York Yankee batted safely from May 15 to July 16, 1941, in a total of fifty-six games. Most people believe that record will last for a long time.

Which two National League pitchers won the Cy Young Award three times?

Sandy Koufax and Tom Seaver.

Who scored the most points in his rookie season as a professional hockey player?

Bryan Trottier scored 94 points while playing for the New York Islanders in the 1975–1976 season.

Who was the last college athlete to make All American in both football and basketball?

Otto Graham was an All American basketball and football player at Northwestern University in 1943–1944.

Dorothy Hamill

True or false? Dorothy Hamill is a world champion swimmer.

False. She is a world champion ice skater.

35

Jackie Robinson was the first black American to play major-league baseball. Which team did he play for?

The Brooklyn Dodgers.

True or false? Willie Mosconi was a champion pocket-billiards player.

True.

Willy Mosconi

Which professional football player caught the most touchdown passes?

Don Hutson, playing for the Green Bay Packers, caught 99 touchdown passes between 1935 and 1945.

The Sullivan Award is given to the outstanding amateur athlete each year. Who won it in 1976?

Bruce Jenner, the Decathlon champion of the 1976 Olympics.

The Female Athlete of the Year Award of the Associated Press was given to an American tennis player in 1974. Who was she?

Chris Evert, a great tennis player.

In 1977 Muhammed Ali was rated number-one heavyweight fighter in the world. Who were number two and number three?

Number two was George Forman, and number three was Ken Norton.

Muhammed Ali

In the last five years, one college football team has won the Rose Bowl three times. Is that team Southern California, UCLA, Michigan, or Ohio State?

The answer is Southern California. Southern California beat Ohio State in the 1973 Rose Bowl, 42 to 17, Ohio State in the 1975 Rose Bowl, 18 to 17, and Michigan in 1977, 14 to 6.

Leo Durocher was a great manager for the Brooklyn Dodgers. Did he ever manage any other New York team?

Leo Durocher was also the manager of the New York Giants, winners of the National League pennant in 1951 and 1954.

Which baseball player holds the record for receiving the most bases on balls in one season?

Babe Ruth was walked 170 times in the 1923 season.

Which professional football player gained the most yards in 1976?

O.J. Simpson, playing for Buffalo, gained 1,503 yards that year.

True or false? The great horse War Admiral won the Triple Crown.

True. War Admiral won the Kentucky Derby, the Preakness, and the Belmont Stakes in 1937.

Who is the all-time winning harness-race driver?

William Haughton.

Johnny Unitas

True or false? John Unitas holds the record for most touchdown passes during his career.

True. John Unitas threw 290 touchdown passes.

True or false? The first Winter Olympic Games were held in Montreal, Canada.

False. The first Winter Olympic Games were held in Chamonix, France, in 1924.

Which professional hockey team had the longest winning streak?

The Boston Bruins, who won fourteen straight games from December 3, 1929, through January 9, 1930.

Which golfer won the Masters Golf Tournament five times?

On April 13, 1975, Jack Nicklaus won his fifth Masters Golf Tournament at Augusta, Georgia.

James Papreck of Northbrook, Illinois, took the world barrel-jumping championship for the third time on January 15, 1977. How many barrels did he jump?

The champ made it over 16 barrels, jumping a total distance of 26 feet 10¾ inches.

John McGraw was a great baseball manager. Can you name the team he managed?

McGraw, manager of the New York Giants, led his team to National League pennants in 1904, 1905, 1911, 1912, 1913, 1917, 1921, 1922, 1923, 1924.

John McGraw

Can you name the first black football player ever to win the Heisman Trophy?

Ernie Davis of Syracuse was awarded the Heisman Trophy as the best college football player in 1961.

In 1911, Ray Harroun won the first Indianapolis 500 championship. Can you guess how fast he went? Was it 74.59 MPH, 82.47 MPH, or 98 MPH?

Driving in a racing car called the Marmon Wasp, Ray Harroun achieved a speed of 74.59 MPH in the 1911 Indianapolis 500.

On November 8, 1970, Tom Dempsey went into the record books. Do you know why?

Tom Dempsey kicked the longest field goal—63 yards in a game between New Orleans and Detroit.

Can you name the college football player who scored the most points in one game? Here is a hint: he played for Syracuse University, went on to become a great professional football player, and then a famous movie actor.

Did you guess Jim Brown? He scored 43 points for Syracuse in 1956.

True or false? Hack Wilson, the great Chicago Cub center fielder, batted in more runs in one season than any other baseball player in history.

True. Hack Wilson had 190 RBI's for the Chicago Cubs in 1930.

Hack Wilson

Which professional basketball team had the most consecutive victories in a single season?

The Los Angeles Lakers won thirty-three consecutive games during the 1971—1972 season.

True or false? Professional basketball courts measure 100 by 65 feet.

False. They measure 94 by 50 feet.

Babe Ruth

When Babe Ruth retired from the New York Yankees everybody remembered the number he had on his uniform. Was it number 2, number 7, or number 12?

When he was playing for the New York Yankees the Babe's number was 3. When he retired, his number was retired as well.

Who was the first designated hitter ever to hit a home run? Was it Willie Mays, Mickey Mantle, Johnny Bench, or Tony Oliva?

Did you guess Tony Oliva? That was right.

43

Patty Costello was Woman of the Year in what sport in 1976? Golf, bowling, or track?

Patty Costello of Scranton, Pennsylvania, was Woman Bowler of the Year for 1976.

Patty Costello

Which professional sport has a two-minute warning?

Football.

At the 1972 Olympics the Russians won the basketball championship. Who won in 1976?

The basketball team from the United States won the Olympic championship that year.

A professional basketball player named Johnny Kerr is a record beater. Do you know why?

Johnny Kerr played in the most consecutive professional basketball games, a total of 844, between October 31, 1954, and November 4, 1965.

Willie Mays was named the Most Valuable Player in the National League twice. Name the two years for which he received the award.

Willie Mays was the National League's Most Valuable Player in 1954 and 1965.

How many gold medals did Mark Spitz win in the 1972 Olympics?

Mark Spitz's swimming accomplishments earned him seven gold medals in the 1972 Olympics.

Mark Spitz

See if you can name the professional football player who scored the most points in a single game?

Ernie Nevers scored 40 points in a game between the Chicago Cardinals and the Chicago Bears on November 28, 1929. He scored 6 touchdowns and 4 points after touchdown.

Which was the last horse to win racing's Triple Crown?

When Seattle Slew won the Belmont Stakes on June 11, 1977, he became the tenth horse to win thoroughbred racing's Triple Crown. The other horses to win it were Sir Barton in 1919, Gallant Fox in 1930, Omaha in 1935, War Admiral in 1937, Whirlaway in 1941, Count Fleet in 1943, Assault in 1946, Citation in 1948, and Secretariat in 1973.

In 1976, Mike Schmidt was the National League's leading home-run hitter with 38 homers. Who was the leading home-run hitter in the American League that year?

Craig Nettles, of the New York Yankees, who hit 32 home runs.

Name the outstanding American swimmer who received a gold medal at the 1976 Olympics for the 100-meter backstroke and the 200-meter backstroke.

John Naber.

True or false? The great basketball player Rick Barry plays the position of guard.

False. Rick Barry plays forward for the Golden State Warriors.

Who was the college basketball player who scored the most points in a single game?

In a college game between Furman and Newberry on February 13, 1954, Frank Selby scored 100 points.

What man served the longest as a college football coach? Was it Knute Rockne?

No. Amos Alonzo Stagg was a college football coach for fifty-seven years. He was the football coach for Springfield College, University of Chicago, and College of the Pacific.

True or false? The light welterweight gold-medal winner at the 1976 Summer Olympics was Ray Leonard.

True. Ray Leonard, the exciting fighter from the United States, was the light-welterweight gold-medal winner at the 1976 Olympics.

Leon Spinks won a gold medal for the United States in the light-heavyweight division at the same Olympics.

Johnny Bench is a great baseball player. Which team does Johnny Bench play for?

Johnny Bench is the star catcher for the Cincinnati Reds.

The first professional basketball All-Star game was played in 1951. The West won that first All-Star game. Is that true or false?

False. The East beat the West with a score of 111 to 94.

Who was the first professional golfer to win over $100,000 in a single year?

Arnold Palmer won $128,230 in 1963.

Joe Namath was the quarterback for the New York Jets. What team does he play for now?

The Los Angeles Rams.

Can you name the only baseball player who scored 6 runs in a game two times?

That record belongs to Mel Ott. He did it the first time on August 4, 1934, and again on April 30, 1944.

Julius Erving was the Most Valuable Player in the American Basketball Association for three years. Name the years.

Julius Erving, or "Doctor J," as he is called, was American Basketball Association MVP in the 1974 and 1976 seasons. In 1975 he shared the award with George McGinnis.

Julius Erving

Name the big-league pitcher who holds the record for the most shutouts during his career.

Walter Johnson, while pitching for Washington from 1907 to 1927, had 113 shutouts.

Dave Roberts holds the record for the pole vault. How high did he jump?

In a pole-vault jump that took place on March 28, 1975, in Gainesville, Florida, Dave Roberts cleared 18 feet 6½ inches. The former Rice University student broke the record of 18 feet 5¾ inches that had been set by Bob Seagren on July 2, 1972.

Dave Roberts

Since 1960, three Americans have won the Decathlon at the Olympic Games. Can you name two out of three?

Rafer Johnson won the 1960 Decathlon. William Toomey won the 1968 Decathlon. The American winner in 1976 was Bruce Jenner. He scored a record of 8,618 points.

Which country has won the most gold medals in the Olympic games from 1896 to 1976?

The United States has won 620 gold medals. The Soviet Union is second with 271, and Great Britain is third with 147.

Which college football team won the very first Rose Bowl game?

Michigan beat Stanford 49 to 0 in the first Rose Bowl game in 1902.

Which basketball player had the highest scoring average in one season during the American Basketball Association play-offs?

Rick Barry, playing for Washington in the 1969–1970 play-offs, averaged 40.14 points.

Rick Barry

Which brothers are considered the greatest winning pitchers in baseball history?

Gaylord and Jim Perry, who have won more than four hundred games between them.

True or false? A professional football game has never been postponed because of weather.

True.

The pitcher who had the most consecutive strike-outs in an All-Star game was Tom Seaver. True or false?

False. Carl Hubbell of the New York Giants, playing in an All-Star game on July 10, 1934, struck out five American League batters in a row.

Which was the first baseball team to turn professional?

The Cincinnati Red Stockings, in 1869. In that year the captain of their team was guaranteed $2,000.

In the five matches held between 1972 and 1976 the championships at Wimbledon were won by only two women. Who were they?

Billie Jean King won the Wimbledon championship in 1972, 1973, and 1975. Chris Evert won it in 1974 and 1976.

Which major-league baseball team was once known as "The Gashouse Gang"?

The St. Louis Cardinals were named "The Gas House Gang" in 1935.

Rod Laver is a great professional tennis player. Is he left-handed or right-handed?

Laver is a lefty.

Rod Laver

Has there ever been a left-handed catcher in major-league baseball?

In 1900 a left-hander named Jack Clements retired after catching in 1,100 games. More recently, in 1958, a left-hander named Dale Long caught 2 games for the Chicago Cubs. They were the only two left-handed catchers in the majors.

Which of the following is not a major-league baseball player? (1) Tom Seaver; (2) Earl Monroe; (3) Rusty Staub; (4) Pete Rose.

Earl Monroe is a basketball player for the New York Knicks.

Which baseball player is nicknamed "The Bird"?

Mark Fidrych, a sensational pitcher for the Detroit Tigers.

Who was the first American to win the marathon race in the Olympics since 1908?

Frank Shorter, a graduate of Yale University, won the marathon in the 1972 Olympics, which were held in Munich, Germany.

Which two baseball players made the most hits in a single game?

Wilbert Robinson got 7 hits for Baltimore in the National League on June 10, 1892, and Rennie Stennett got 7 hits for Pittsburgh in the National League on September 16, 1975.

Who was the only baseball player to pitch a no-hit game in his very first game in the major leagues?

Bobo Holloman of the St. Louis Browns in 1953.

Pistol Pete Maravich scored the most points of any college basketball player. How many points did he score?

Playing for Louisiana State University between 1967 and 1970, Pete Maravich scored 3,667 points.

Can you name the pitcher who won the most games in one season?

Way back in 1884 Hoss Radbourne won sixty games for Providence in the National League.

Who was the Professional Rodeo Cowboys' Association's 1976 all-around champion?

Tom Ferguson of Miami, Oklahoma, who won the award for the third year in a row.

How long is a polo field?

Polo is played on a 300 by 160 yard field.

Which were the last two cities to have baseball teams in the American League?

There are now fourteen teams in the American League. The last two cities to join it were Toronto and Seattle in 1977.

True or false? The East won the All-Star professional basketball games in 1975 and 1976.

True. The East beat the West in the NBA All-Star game of 1975 by a score of 108 to 102; in 1976 the East won by 123 to 109.

Which catcher was the Most Valuable Player in the American League in 1976?

Thurman Munson, of the New York Yankees. In 1976 Thurman Munson drove in 105 runs for the New York Yankees and had a batting average of .302.

Which professional basketball player holds the record for the most free throws without a miss?

Bob Pettit made 19 free throws in a row in a game against the Boston Celtics on November 22, 1961, while playing for the St. Louis Hawks.

When did a driver first go over 100 miles per hour in the Indianapolis 500? Was it 1921, 1925, or 1938?

In 1925 Pete DePaolo recorded a speed of 101.13 MPH in the Indianapolis 500.

Who was the home-run slugger who broke Babe Ruth's record of 714 home runs?

Hank Aaron, of the Atlanta Braves, broke the Babe's record on April 8, 1974, when he hit home-run number 715.

True or false? National League teams have won more World Series than American League teams.

False. As of 1976 American League teams won forty-three World Series and National League teams won thirty.

Can you name the professional fighter who scored the most knockouts during his professional boxing career?

Light-heavyweight Archie Moore knocked out 136 opponents during his long boxing career.

The manager of the New York Yankees in 1977 was Leo Durocher. True or false?

False. Billy Martin was the manager of the Yankees in 1977.

In horseshoe pitching, how far away should the metal stake be? Is it 30 feet, 40 feet, or 50 feet?

Forty feet.

In 1952, Richard Button achieved a great accomplishment. Do you know what it was?

In that year Richard Button, an American, won the men's world figure-skating championship.

Richard Button

Do you know the name of the professional basketball player who holds the record for the most assists in one season? Was it Jerry West, Nate Archibald, or Johnny Kerr?

If you said Nate Archibald you were right. Playing for KC–Omaha in the 1972–1973 season, Nate Archibald had 910 assists.

Which racing trainer had the most horses win the Kentucky Derby?

Ben Jones. He had six Kentucky Derby winners—1938, Lawrin; 1941, Whirlaway; 1944, Pensive; 1948, Citation; 1949, Ponder; and in 1952, Hill Gail.

What movie star is also known for his achievements as a race-car driver? Is it Dustin Hoffman, Robert Redford, Paul Newman, or Jack Nicholson?

Paul Newman is not only a fine actor but he has also driven in many auto races.

When was the first World Series game played?

A World Series game was held in 1903. Boston (AL) won, with five against Pittsburgh's (NL) three. The first official World Series game was held in 1905. In that game the New York Giants of the National League beat the Philadelphia Athletics of the American League, winning four games to the Athletics' one.

True or false? The National League was founded before the American League.

True. The National League was founded in 1876, the American League in 1900.

Which college football player scored the most points in a college game?

In a game between Syracuse and Colgate on November 17, 1956, Jim Brown scored 43 points for Syracuse. The great football player scored 6 touchdowns and 7 points after touchdown.

A captain in the United States Air Force won a gold medal for springboard diving at the 1972 Olympics. Do you know who it was?

Captain Micki King won the gold medal for women's springboard diving at the 1972 Olympics.

In 1975 and 1976 the same National League team won the World Series. Name that team.

The Cincinnati Reds beat the Boston Red Sox in the 1975 World Series, four games to three; and Cincinnati beat the New York Yankees in the 1976 World Series four games to none.

True or false? Nolan Ryan had the most major-league strike-outs in one season.

True. In 1973 Nolan Ryan struck out 383 batters.

Only one professional quarterback completed more than 70 percent of his passes in one season. Who was it?

Sammy Baugh, the great quarterback for the Washington Redskins, successfully completed 128 out of 182 passes during the 1945 season.

Name the horse who won more money in racing than any other horse. Was it Secretariat, Kelso, or Foolish Pleasure?

Kelso won $1,977,896, an all-time record.

In his first year of pitching in the major leagues, Mark (The Bird) Fidrych, won nineteen games. True or false?

True. Pitching his first season in the major leagues in 1976 for the Detroit Tigers, The Bird won nineteen games and lost nine, leading the American League with an ERA of 2.34.

Joe DiMaggio

How many years did Joe DiMaggio win the American League batting championship? Was it two years, three years, or five years?

Joe DiMaggio was the American League's leading hitter for two years. In 1939 he led the league with a batting average of .381 while playing for the New York Yankees, and in 1940 DiMaggio led the American League with a batting average of .352.

Who was the first second-baseman to be voted the Most Valuable Player in the National League?

Frank Frisch, while playing second base for St. Louis in 1931. The first second baseman to win the Most Valuable Player Award in the American League was Charles L. Gehringer, who played second base for Detroit in 1937.

Everybody remembers Joe DiMaggio, the great baseball player, but what are the names of his brothers, who also played baseball?

Joe's brothers are Dom, who played eleven seasons with the Boston Red Sox, and Vince, who played ten seasons with five different National League teams.

Which yacht won the American Cup race in 1967 and 1970?

In 1967 *Intrepid* beat *Dame Pattie,* of Australia, 4 races to 0, and in 1970 *Intrepid* beat *Gretel II,* of Australia, 4 races to 1.

Which professional football team won the most league championships?

Green Bay. The Green Bay Wisconsin team won eleven league championships.

On April 16, 1968, the Houston Astros played the New York Mets in a game that went down in history. What happened?

It took 24 innings for the Houston Astros to beat the New York Mets in the longest 1-run shutout in baseball history.

Which professional basketball team had the longest losing streak?

In 1973 the Philadelphia 76ers lost twenty games in a row.

The movie "The Great White Hope" was based on the life story of what great prize fighter? Was it Muhammed Ali, Joe Louis, or Jack Johnson?

The great Jack Johnson.

Muhammed Ali   Jack Johnson   Joe Louis

When was the last time a National League pitcher won thirty games?

In 1934, when Dizzy Dean had a record of thirty wins and seven losses.

When was our National Anthem first played at a major-league baseball game?

When the fans stood for the seventh-inning stretch of the opening game of the 1918 World Series between Boston and Chicago, the band started to play "The Star Spangled Banner."

Who was the first professional football player to rush for more than 2,000 yards in one season?

During the 1973 season O.J. Simpson, of the Buffalo Bills, rushed for 2,003 yards.

Who was the youngest pitcher ever to be elected to the Baseball Hall of Fame?

Sandy Koufax, who pitched for the Los Angeles Dodgers, was only thirty-six when he was elected to the Hall of Fame in 1972.

Jimmy Connors

True or false? The leading professional tennis money winner in 1976 was Jimmy Connors.

True. Jimmy Connors won $687,335. Ilie Nastase was second, with a total of $576,705.

Connie Mack was the manager of the Philadelphia Phillies for many years. What was the first year he won an American League championship?

Connie Mack led his team to an American League pennant for the first time in 1902. He won his last American League pennant for Philadelphia in 1931.

Connie Mack

Ralph Kiner was a great home-run hitter for the Pittsburgh Pirates. Do you know how many seasons Kiner led his league in home runs?

Ralph Kiner led the National League in home runs for seven years in a row, from 1946 to 1952.

Which of these famous auto racers won a record twenty-seven major auto races? Was it Al Unser, A.J. Foyt, or Jackie Stewart?

Before he retired in 1973, Jackie Stewart had won twenty-seven major auto races.

Who was the first Most Valuable Player for the American Basketball Association?

Connie Hawkins, of the Pittsburgh Pipers, in the 1967–1968 season. The ABA has since merged with the NBA.

True or false? Famous baseball player Jackie Robinson was once a star football player for the University of Michigan.

False. Jackie Robinson was a star football player for UCLA.

Who was the youngest fighter to become heavyweight champion of the world?

Floyd Patterson was only twenty-one when he knocked out Archie Moore in the fifth round in a fight in Chicago on November 30, 1956.

While playing football for Stamford University between 1968 and 1970, Jim Plunkett gained the most yards for a college football player by passing and rushing. Can you guess how many yards he gained?

He gained 7,887 yards.

Who pitched the only perfect World Series game? Was it Bob Feller, Tom Seaver, or Don Larsen?

Don Larsen pitched a perfect World Series game for the New York Yankees on October 8, 1956. No player of the opposing team reached first base.

Billie Jean King plays tennis for which professional tennis team?

The New York Apples.

The award for Most Valuable Player went to the same professional hockey player in 1975 and 1976. Was it Bobby Orr, Phil Esposito, or Bobby Clarke?

Bobby Clarke, playing for Philadelphia, was named Most Valuable Player, for which he received the Hart Memorial Trophy.

Bobby Orr   *Phil Esposito*   *Bobby Clarke*

From 1972 to 1975 the same hitter led the American League in batting. Who was it?

Rod Carew led the American League in 1972 with a batting average of .318. In 1973 his batting average was .350. In 1974 Carew had a batting average of .364, and in 1975 he led the league with a batting average of .359.

Which professional basketball team won the most games in a single season?

During the 1971–1972 season, the Los Angeles Lakers won sixty-nine games. The team that lost the most games in one season was the Philadelphia 76ers, who lost seventy-three games during the 1972–1973 season.

True or false? The great pitchers Sandy Koufax, of the Los Angeles Dodgers, and Bob Feller, of the Cleveland Indians, never pitched in the minor leagues.

True.

Bob Feller

Sandy Koufax

Who was the last quarterback to win the Heisman Trophy?

Pat Sullivan, of Auburn.

True or false? Bob Gibson holds the record for a pitcher with the lowest earned run average during one season in the National League.

False. Bob Gibson, pitching for St. Louis in 1968, had an ERA of 1.12, but this is only the second-lowest ERA in the National League, the lowest was 0.90 for New York player Ferdinand M. Schupp in 1916.

Who was the youngest baseball player ever to play in the major leagues?

Joe Nuxhall started as pitcher for the Cincinnati team in June 1944, when he was only fifteen years old.

Has an amateur golfer ever won a PGA tournament?

Yes. The winner of the 1976 Canadian Open was Doug Sanders, an amateur at the time.

Patricia McCormick

The same woman won a gold medal for platform diving at both the 1952 and 1956 Olympics. Who was it?

Patricia McCormick.

Cassius Clay changed his name and became one of the greatest fighters of all time. What is his name now?

Muhammed Ali. Ali is a great heavyweight champion.

69

True or false? A Russian athlete won the Decathlon in the 1972 Olympics.

True. Nikolai Avilov, a great Russian athlete, won the Decathlon.

Gordie Howe has scored more goals than any other professional hockey player. Who is the second leading scorer?

Bobby Hull, who scored 604 goals through the 1975-1976 season.

Which basketball player is nicknamed "Dollar Bill"?

Bill Bradley, of the New York Knicks.

Bill Bradley

Mildred "Babe" Didrikson was known as one of the great women golfers of all time. But did you know that Babe Didrikson also won two Olympic gold medals? Which events do you think she won her gold medals for?

In the 1932 Olympics, Babe Didrikson won gold medals for 80-meter hurdles and the javelin.

Babe Didrikson

Name the winner of the 1977 Orange Bowl game.

Ohio State beat Colorado in the 1977 Orange Bowl game, 27 to 10.

Who was the first driver to win the Indianapolis 500 four times?

A.J. Foyt won the Indianapolis 500 in 1961, 1964, 1967, and 1977.

Howard Cosell is: (1) a football player; (2) a sportscaster; (3) a hockey player; (4) a tennis player.

Howard Cosell is the famous sportscaster for ABC on *Monday Night Football*.

Howard Cosell

True or false? Former President Gerald Ford was an assistant football coach at Yale University.

True. President Ford also played football for the University of Michigan in 1932 and 1933.

Which college basketball player holds the record for the most points scored as a college player in one year?

In his senior year at Winston-Salem in 1966–1967 Earl Monroe scored 1,329 points.

Lou Brock

True or false? Lou Brock stole more bases than any other player in one season.

Not quite true. Lou Brock stole the most bases, 118, in games played since 1900, for St. Louis of the National League during the 1974 season. But in 1888 Harry Stovey, of Philadelphia, stole 156 bases.

What was the smallest crowd ever to watch a heavyweight title fight?

Only 2,434 fans turned up to watch the Muhammed Ali–Sonny Liston fight in May, 1965.

True or false? In 1969 the game of baseball was one hundred years old.

True.

Speed skater Sheila Young, from Detroit, won three medals at the 1976 Olympics. What were they?

Ms. Young won a gold medal for the 500-meter race, a silver for the 1500-meter race, and a bronze for the 1000-meter race.

Sheila Young

Which American League pitcher holds the record for the most strike-outs in a single game?

On August 12, 1974, Nolan Ryan struck out nineteen Boston batters while pitching for California. National League pitchers Steven Carlton of St. Louis, playing against New York on September 15, 1969, and Tom Seaver of the New York Mets, against the St. Louis Cardinals on April 22, 1970, also struck out nineteen batters in a single game.

In which year was the game of paddle tennis originated? Was it 1914, 1924, 1926, or 1930?

Paddle tennis started in 1924.

How many passes did football great Johnny Unitas complete?

The great quarterback completed 2,830 passes, ranking second in pass completions.

True or false? Dizzy and Daffy Dean were brothers and major-league baseball players. They were both outfielders.

Part true and part false. Dizzy and Daffy Dean were brothers and baseball players but they were both pitchers.

Dizzy Dean

Daffy Dean

Can you name the professional football player who completed the most passes in one season? Was it Joe Namath, Sonny Jurgensen, or Sammy Baugh?

Sonny Jurgensen, playing quarterback for Washington in 1967, completed 1,288 passes.

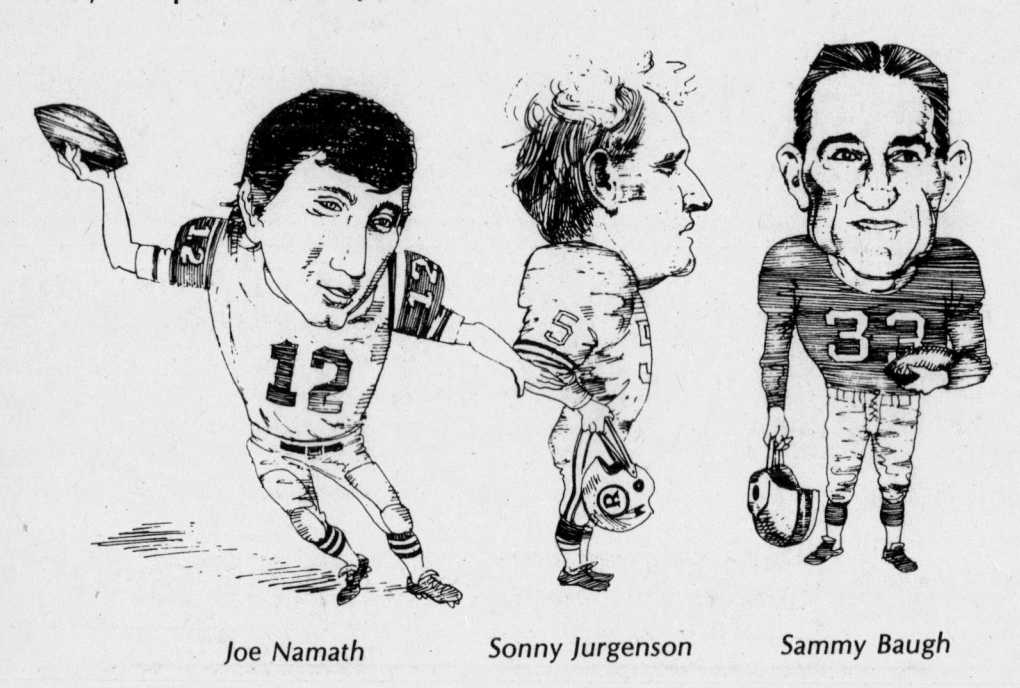

Joe Namath   Sonny Jurgenson   Sammy Baugh

Babe Ruth hit 4 home runs in the 1926 World Series. Has that record ever been beaten?

Yes. Reggie Jackson, playing for the New York Yankees in the 1977 World Series, hit 5 home runs.

Who was the last American League baseball player to win the Triple Crown?

Carl Yastrzemski of the Boston Red Sox. In 1967 he won the Triple Crown with a batting average of .326, the most home runs, 44, and a score of 121 RBI's, the highest in the league.

Which of these professional football players lead the league in field goals the most seasons? Was it Jim Turner, George Blanda, Tom Dempsey, or Lou Groza?

Lou Groza led his league in field goals five times while playing for Cleveland in 1950, 1952, 1953, 1954, and 1957.

True or false? Muhammed Ali was once the light-heavyweight Olympic champion.

True. Ali won the light-heavyweight championship in the 1960 Olympics in Rome.

Which college basketball team won the Ivy League crown most years in a row?

Dartmouth won the title from 1938 to 1944.

Shane Gould was fifteen years old when she competed in the 1972 Olympics. How many gold medals did she win?

Shane Gould, of Australia, won three gold medals for swimming in the 1972 Olympics.

Shane Gould

Stan Musial was a great player for the St. Louis Cardinals. Is it true that he hit more home runs than any other player in All-Star games?

True. Playing in All-Star games between 1948 and 1960, Stan Musial hit 6 home runs.

Rocky Marciano

True or false? Rocky Marciano retired while he was still world's heavyweight boxing champion.

True. When Marciano retired in 1956, he was still heavyweight champion of the world.

In 1975 and 1976 the same major-league baseball player won the Most Valuable Player Award in the National League. Who was it?

Joe Morgan, star second baseman of the Cincinnati Reds, was the National League's Most Valuable Player in 1975 and 1976.

True or false? Baseball player Johnny Bench never won the Most Valuable Player award.

False. Johnny Bench, of the Cincinnati Reds, was the Most Valuable Player in the National League in 1972.

Who was the baseball player who received the most bases on balls?

Babe Ruth received 2,056 bases on balls during his career.

Who was the home-run king in 1976? Was it Mike Schmidt or Dave Kingman?

Mike Schmidt, of the Philadelphia Phillies, led the major league in home runs, with 36 in 1974 and 38 in 1975 and 1976.

Which position did the great soccer player Pele play? Was it forward, midfielder, or defender?

Pele played forward for the New York Cosmos.

Which country won the last three International Badminton championship contests? Was it the United States, the Soviet Union, or Indonesia?

Indonesia took the last three International Badminton championships.

Which professional golfer won the most tournaments in a single season? Was it Jack Nicklaus, Arnold Palmer, or Johnny Miller?

It wasn't any of those three. Byron Nelson won nineteen tournaments in 1945, including the U.S. Open, PGA, and the Canadian Open.

Jerry West

Jerry West was one of the great basketball players of all time. He holds the record for most free throws made in a basketball season. Was the number 610, 840, 900, or 910?

The right answer is 840.

Which rookie goal tender made the record of 15 shutouts in a single National Hockey League season?

Tony Esposito, during the 1969–1970 season.

Who was the first professional woman golfer to earn more than $100,000 in one year?

In 1976 Judy Rankin earned over $100,000 on the woman's golf tour.

True or false? The soccer World Cup winner for 1974 was West Germany.

True. The World Cup winner in the previous competition was Brazil in 1970.

Who was the professional baseball player who completed the only unassisted triple play in a World Series game?

Bill Wambsganss, in the fifth inning of the fifth game, playing for the Cleveland Indians against Brooklyn in the 1920 World Series.

Which professional football player appeared in the most consecutive games?

Jim Marshall played in 236 consecutive games. He played for Cleveland in 1960 and Minnesota from 1961 to 1976.

When was the first Indianapolis 500 auto race held? Was in 1898, 1901, 1911, or 1914?

If you said 1911, you were right. The actual date for that Indianapolis 500 race was May 30, 1911.

How many consecutive games did Lou Gehrig play in before he retired as one of the greatest New York Yankees of all time?

Lou Gehrig's consecutive playing streak started in 1925 for a total of 2,130.

Joe Namath

Who has the record for gaining the most football yards in one season as a quarterback?

Joe Namath, of the New York Jets, passed for 4,007 yards during the 1967 season.

Gordy Howe

Only one man in the history of professional hockey holds the following records: (1) played most seasons; (2) played most games; (3) scored most goals; (4) had most assists; (5) had most points. Who is this great hockey player?

Gordie Howe.

Which was the first American Football League team to win the Super Bowl?

The New York Jets, which defeated Baltimore 16 to 7 in the 1969 Super Bowl game.

The United States won the gold medal for basketball in the 1976 Olympics. Which country won the gold medal for basketball in the 1972 Olympics?

The Soviet Union.

When was the first time a sports announcer gave a play-by-play account of a World Series game over the radio?

In 1921 Harold Arlin broadcast the World Series game over Pittsburgh radio station KDKA.

Can you name the most popular sport in the world?

Soccer. The game is played and watched by enthusiasts all over the world.

Hal Greer

Can you name the professional basketball player who made the most fouls during his basketball career?

Hal Greer committed 3,855 fouls while playing for the Syracuse Nationals and the Philadelphia 76ers.

84

Nadia Comenechi

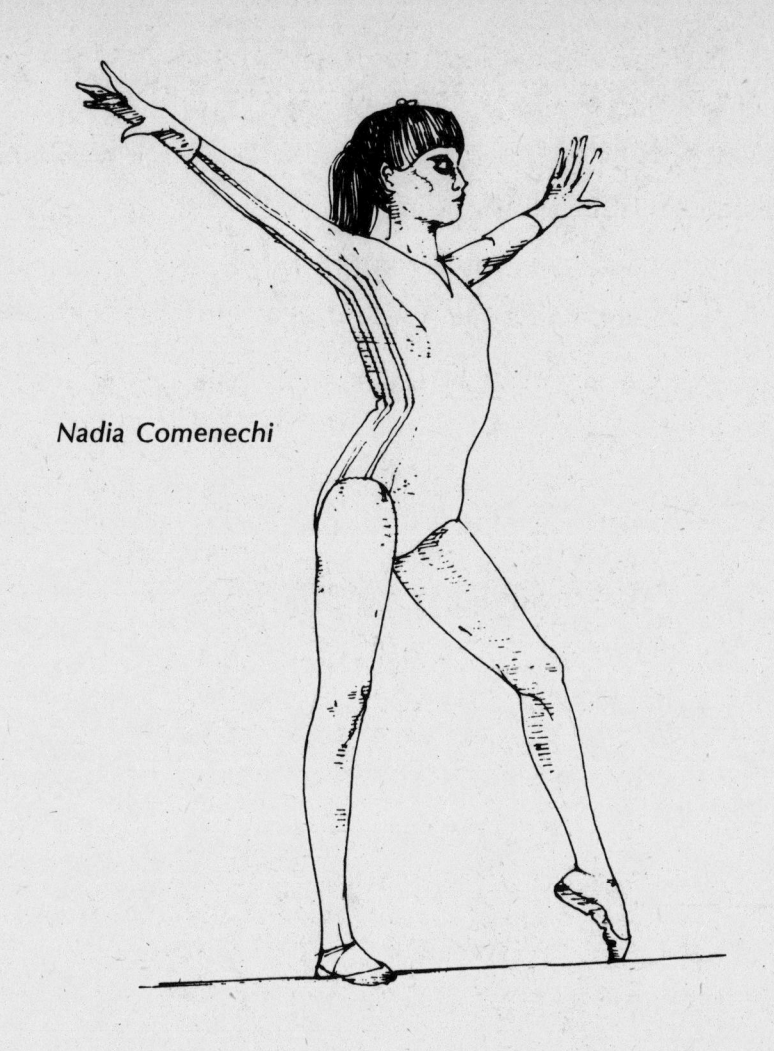

At the 1976 Summer Olympics, which woman won a gold medal for the best all-around performance in gymnastics?

Nadia Comaneci, of Romania, with an astonishing 79.275 points.

Which professional football player holds the record for most field goals kicked in a single game?

Jim Bakken kicked 7 field goals for the St. Louis Cardinals in a game against the Pittsburgh Steelers in 1967.

Norm Van Brocklin, once the quarterback for the Los Angeles Rams, went into the record books on September 28, 1951. Do you know why?

During a game between Los Angeles and New York Norm Van Brocklin gained the most yards passing in a single game—554 yards.

Norm Van Brocklin

The 1976 Winter Olympics were held at Innsbruck, Austria. How many gold medals did the United States win?

The United States placed third with three gold medals. East Germany placed second with seven gold medals, and the Soviet Union placed first with thirteen.

The United States has never won a team gold medal for fencing at the Olympics. True or false?

True. West Germany won the gold medal for team fencing at the 1976 Olympics, and the team from Poland won the gold medal at the 1972 Olympics.

Arnold Palmer   Walter Hagen

Can you name the professional golfer who won four PGA championships in a row? Was it Arnold Palmer or Walter Hagen?

Walter Hagen won four PGA championships in a row, from 1924 to 1927. He won a total of five PGA championships.

Which breed of dog was the Westminster Kennel Club's Best in Show in 1976?

A Lakeland Terrier owned by Mrs. Virginia K. Dickson was Best in Show for 1976.

Yogi Berra

True or false? Yogi Berra was once the manager of the New York Mets.

True. Yogi Berra's New York Mets were the National League Champions in 1973.

True or false? George Sisler, of the old St. Louis Browns, holds the record for the most base hits for one person?

True. George Sisler got 257 base hits in 1920.

Who was the very first man to run the mile in under 4 minutes?

Roger Bannister of Great Britain ran the mile in 3:59:4 in 1954. The first American to run the mile in under 4 minutes was Jim Ryun in 1966. His time was 3:51:3.

Each of two jockeys rode five Kentucky Derby winners. Who were they?

Bill Hartack and Eddie Arcaro.

Jerry West   Wilt Chamberlain   Walt Frazier

Which professional basketball player scored the most points in his career in the basketball play-offs? Was it Jerry West, Wilt Chamberlain, or Walt Frazier?

Jerry West, playing for the Los Angeles Lakers, scored 4,457 points in play-off games between 1961 and 1974.

Rudy York hit the most home runs in one month. Did he hit 18 home runs, 20, 15, or 8?

During August, 1937, Rudy York hit 18 home runs for the Detroit Tigers.

What is the fastest sport in the world?

Skydiving. Free-fall speeds of 614 MPH have been recorded in skydiving competitions.

In 1977 a woman raced in the Indianapolis 500 for the first time. What was her name?

Janet Guthrie, of New York, made racing history when she became the first woman to race in the famous Indianapolis 500 on May 29, 1977. Ms. Guthrie finished twenty-ninth in a field of thirty-three.

Who was the first black quarterback to play in the National Football League?

Willie Thrower of the Chicago Bears in 1953.

Wilt Chamberlain is one of the great athletes of all time. Which sport is he famous for? Football, basketball, tennis, or hockey?

If you said basketball, you were right.

Who was the last National League baseball player to win his league's Triple Crown?

Ducky Medwick did it for the St. Louis Cardinals in 1937.

Name the professional football player who scored the most points in his rookie season.

Gale Sayers scored 22 touchdowns for 132 points in his first year, playing for Chicago in 1965.

Who won the 1976 Associated Press Male Athlete of the Year Award?

Bruce Jenner.

In a baseball game between Oakland and Chicago on September 19, 1972, a record was broken. Do you know what the record was?

In that American League game, Oakland used thirty players against Chicago, the most players ever used by one team in one game.

Johnny Miller

Lee Trevino   Gary Player

In 1971 and 1972 the same golfer won the British Open. Was it Johnny Miller, Gary Player, or Lee Trevino?

Lee Trevino.

Which basketball league used a red, white, and blue basketball?

The teams of the American Basketball Association, which was founded in 1967 and merged with the National Basketball Association in 1976.

Owen Wilson is in the baseball record books. Do you know why?

Playing for Pittsburgh in 1912, Owen Wilson hit 36 three-base hits. A record!

Who was the oldest heavyweight champion fighter?

Jersey Joe Walcott was thirty-eight in 1952, when he was finally defeated as heavyweight champion of the world by Rocky Marciano.

True or false? On a professional baseball diamond the distance between the batter's box and the pitcher's mound is 70 feet.

False. The correct distance is 60 feet, 6 inches.

Who was the professional hockey player who scored the most goals in one game?

Joe Malone, playing for the Quebec Bulldogs, scored 7 goals against Toronto on January 31, 1920.

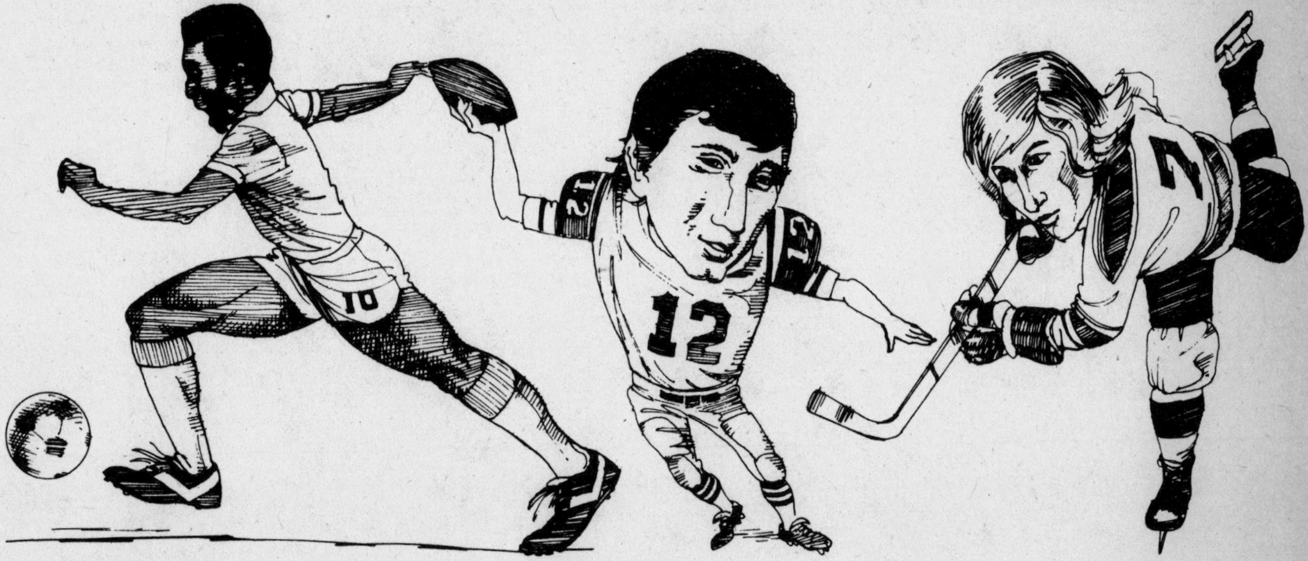

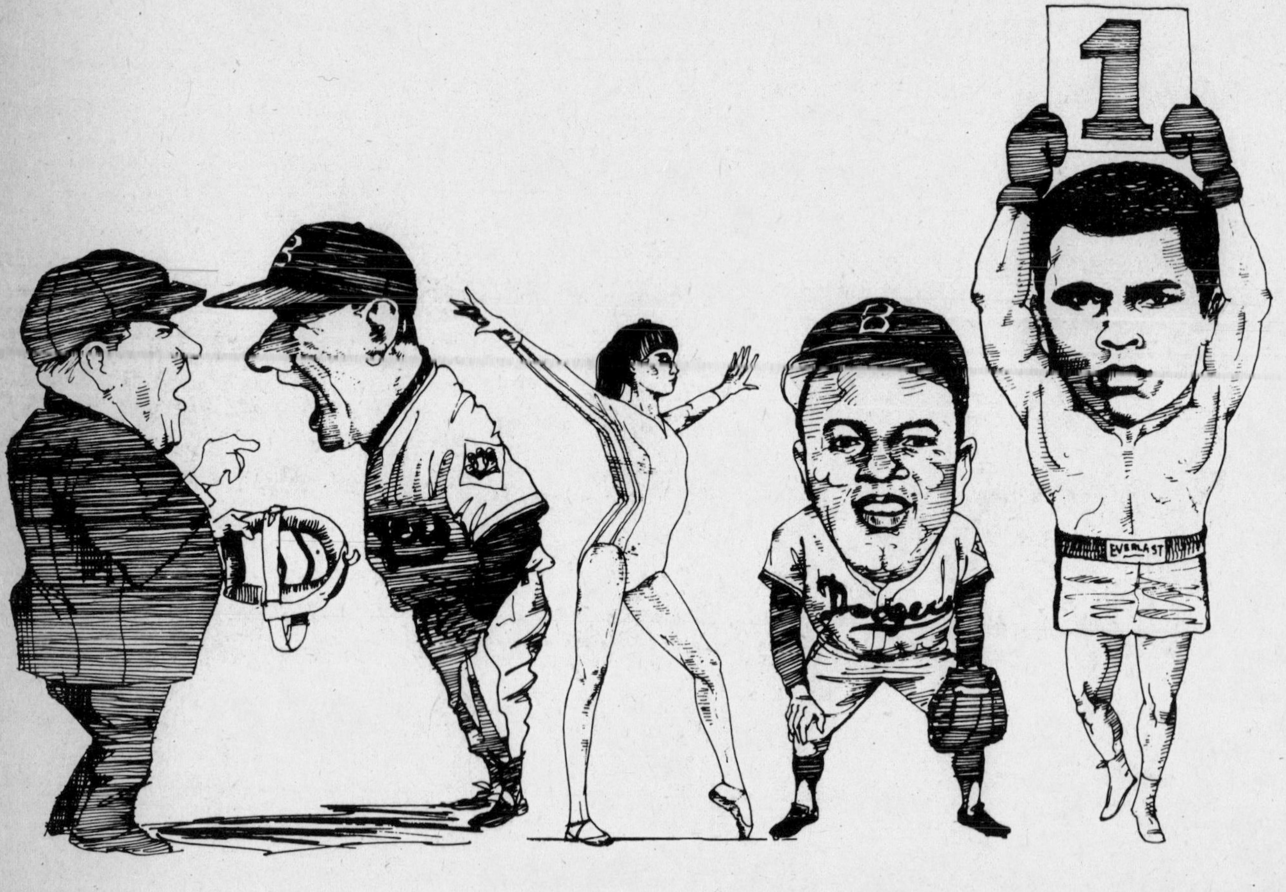
1
EVERLAST

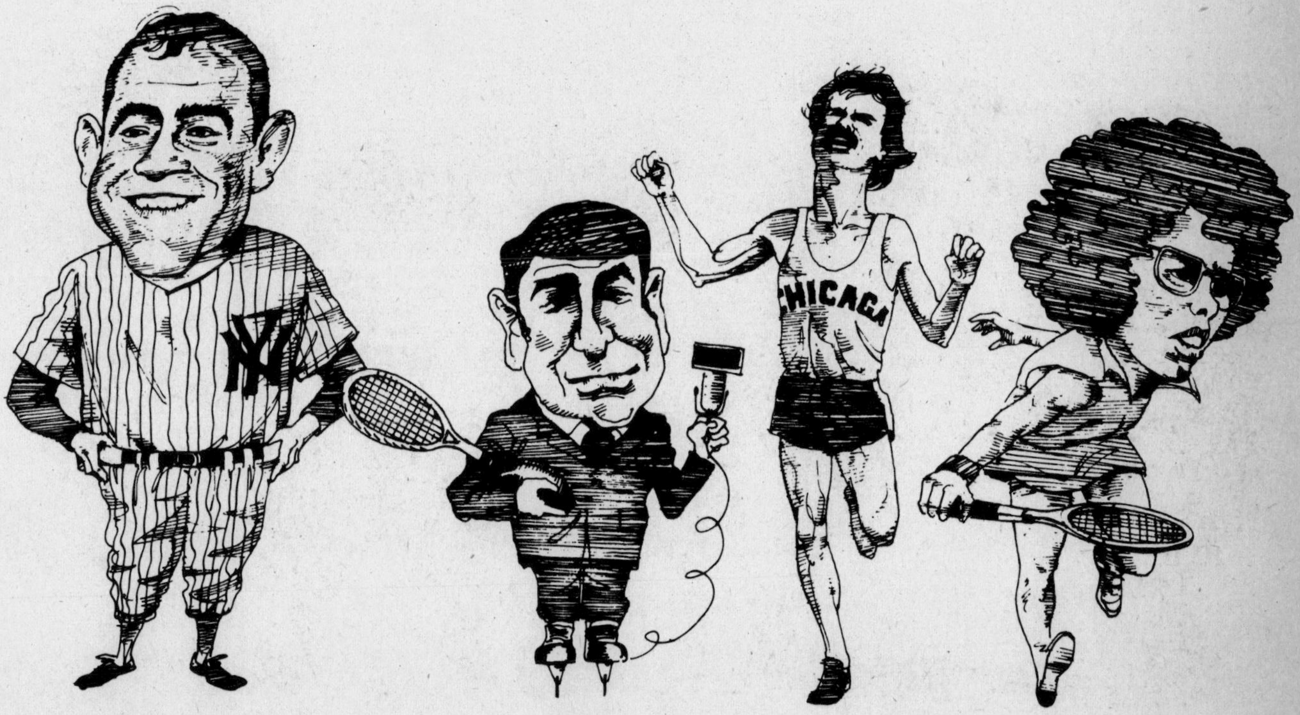
CHICAGO